The Lightness of Reprieve

poems by

Marilyn T. Hedgpeth

Finishing Line Press
Georgetown, Kentucky

The Lightness of Reprieve

Copyright © 2024 by Marilyn T. Hedgpeth
ISBN 979-8-88838-455-8 First Edition
All rights reserved under International and Pan-American Copyright Conventions. No part of this book may be reproduced in any manner whatsoever without written permission from the publisher, except in the case of brief quotations embodied in critical articles and reviews.

ACKNOWLEDGMENTS

In gratitude, to my wonderful family for their support: husband, Hedge, who has always encouraged me to spend more time writing; and to our delightful children and grandchildren, who continue to provide fodder for many wonderings put to paper. Furthermore, I could not have done this without the wisdom and craft of my poetry group that meets weekly: Paul Deblinger, Alan Basting, and Bruce Metge. And lastly, I wish to honor my dear friend, Tricia Jones (and husband, Don), whose brave and valiant battle with pancreatic cancer inspired most of these poems. For friendship, its power to strengthen and encourage, provide solace and bring joy, I am deeply grateful.

Publisher: Leah Huete de Maines
Editor: Christen Kincaid
Cover and Interior Art: Marilyn T. Hedgpeth
Author Photo: Marilyn T. Hedgpeth
Cover Design: Elizabeth Maines McCleavy

Order online: www.finishinglinepress.com
also available on amazon.com

Author inquiries and mail orders:
Finishing Line Press
PO Box 1626
Georgetown, Kentucky 40324
USA

Contents

Mirror Images 1

She Recites a Poem 2

Okra Hope 3

Today, It's Been a Year 5

Tomatoes for the Baby 6

Visiting My Friend 7

The Professor's Cat 9

After Chemo 10

Measuring Love 11

H-O-P-E 12

Handful of Tomatoes 13

First Frost 15

The Lightness of Reprieve 16

Attending to Grief 17

Last Leaf 18

Found in a Forest 20

Crack in My Windshield 21

Mementoes 22

Moravian Star 23

*To friendship,
its power to strengthen and encourage,
provide solace and bring joy.
Our friend, Tricia Jones, was incredibly brave
in her battle with pancreatic cancer.
It was a privilege and pleasure to walk
beside her and husband Don,
to share the weight of that disease, and offer hope.
Friendship was a vital element of her care.
She is the inspiration for this collection.*

*If you are so moved by these poems,
please consider a donation
to PanCAN, (info@pancan.org)
whose vision is to create a world in which
all patients with cancer will thrive.*

\-   *Marilyn*

Mirror Images

Sliding into a booth,
leather cool to my legs,
we take menus in hand;
we glance around,
tempted by lavish meals
rising before other patrons.
An adjacent mirrored wall
makes the tavern seem
twice its size, twice as lively.

Across smooth Formica,
you sip ice water,
watching as your doppleganger
tucks a wayward wisp of hair
into her head-scarf.
Maybe that's an alternate universe,
you say, and this table,
our point of intersection.
Maybe while we grow older,
grayer, wiser perhaps,
they grow younger,
healthier, more vital and able.

We toast to what's possible,
to friendship, regardless.
Condensation drips from our tumblers,
while frost still clings to those
of our glassy companions.

She Recites a Poem

In Time of Silver Rain,
her son memorized
in the fourth grade,
her hands dancing with signs
she contrived to help him
remember each line.
She touches her wrist, for *time*;
wiggles fingers down for *rain*,
up for green grasses growing;
extends her right arm, *of life,*
left, *of life,*
then both outwards, *of life,*
as if embracing it all.

At this shimmering moment,
even as life flows out from her,
she is radiant,
having poured all of herself
into her children;
from her deep well, filling theirs,
extending her right arm,
then left, then both outwards,
as if embracing all
of life,
of life,
of life.

**In Time of Silver Rain*, Langston Hughes

Okra Hope

Ignore it,
the farmers' market vendor tells me
as I admire her ample cartons
crammed with ramrod-straight okra pods.
If you're too nice to it, it won't produce.

Its roots run deep to Africa's searing heat,
sun-bleached clods of dirt and dung
worked by calloused hands,
to gumbo and Gullah climes
where it adapted,
thrived in spite, not because, of us.

When other summer crops wither
on the vine,
it raises its own leafy shade,
its camera lens-like blossom,
points its slender fingers skyward,
honors the heat, the homeland,
the hands, the fuzz and seeds,
that have created its ingestible
earthy resilience.

Today, It's Been a Year

since I penciled in your name,
adding it to the calendar I keep
as a ledger for God's business.

I remember your husband's call,
the announcement that he had
bad news to share,
his voice breaking as he told us.
(You, totally silent,
perhaps tearing up
just to his side.)
Stunned and numb,
I recall sitting on the sofa,
fingering the knotted fringe
on our afghan
as if it were a prayer shawl.

Tomatoes for the Baby

Your husband planted them after Mother's Day:
green zebras, variegated heirlooms,
blood-red beefsteaks, Cherokee purples;
watched the orbs ripen daily,
eager to pick and slice them
so the baby could finger
their seediness.
She touches them to her tongue,
paints her tray, her hair,
makes you laugh.

Stats from Monday's scan,
markers tripling since last time.
He sees the report, keeps results to himself.
You see it too, say nothing,
neither wanting to upset the other;
love unspoken.

Instead, you croon
about the luscious lobes growing,
ripening in the garden
behind the house,
and your first grandchild, tottering
on bare feet from chair to chair.

Visiting My Friend

Willow thin,
skin and eyes translucent,
allowing your inner life to shine;
you seem a fragile figurine,
one I want to hold, but can't,
to take home and keep.
Do you look wonderful,
or do I just feel wonderful
seeing you, hearing your voice,
after all these months of chemo
and quarantine?

I considered bringing cut wildflowers,
but their heads might droop too soon;
sharing pictures of growing grandchildren,
but felt the hint of tomorrow, ephemeral;
even sharing a poem, too poignant,
since most speak of love or death.
Instead, I brought fresh strawberries,
picked yesterday, perfect today,
and we sit on your porch watching
goldfinches flit from sun to shade.

The Professor's Cat

Peeking between bedroom curtains
in pre-dawn's first light, I spot her,
silhouetted in the neighbor's window,
waiting for me to return her marble gaze.
I point her out to my waking grandsons, saying,
There's that professor's cat, watching us!
Again, at moonrise, as they throw off their shoes,
she is still there, sphinx-like, noting
each foot-strike of our comings and goings
across the driveway's divide.
Does she ever sleep, they ask; or move?
Would she miss us if we didn't stare back?
Oddly, I take comfort in being noticed,
watched over, even guarded, perhaps,
if only by a cat.

After Chemo

Eyes, brighter than I recall,
you comment on everything,
as if seeing anew for the last time:
a damask wallpaper pattern,
unfamiliar birds at the feeder,
the outlandish alabaster
bloom of azaleas in our backyard.
We enjoy a meal together,
laughing so much that you
forget to take your pill.

Around that table,
things seem abnormally normal;
while just beneath, hungry cells
continue to feed.
We hug as you leave;
hug too long, not long enough
as you climb into your car.
Just beyond, banks of azaleas
spread a white pall.

Measuring Love

With time so precious,
he begins to lace
his language with fractions:
for breakfast,
half a bowl of oatmeal,
an ounce or two of applesauce,
three-fourths a cup of orange juice.
Everything once whole,
now diminishing; he meters
the inverse of the immeasurable.

At lunch time he rejoices
over three bites of spaghetti,
half a muffin, and her favorite
cup of vanilla ice cream
before napping, off and on
for two-thirds of the afternoon.

Later, he notes she swallows
her pills, one by one
with half a glass of milk
before dozing while holding his hand
at a quarter past eight.
Outside, as deer slide into shadows,
the moon wanes to quarter.

H-O-P-E

He labors down the stairs,
two suitcases in hand, a tangle
of mussed sheets under one arm.
"I don't know why he's doing that,"
his wife whispers to me.
"Round two of treatments
begins next week;
we'll be back."

He works the math on a napkin,
weighing probabilities.

She eats English muffins for breakfast
because the package says,
Wake up to what's possible!

I fingerspell a four-letter word to her.
Outside, a hummingbird
hovers at the feeder,
hoping to perch.

Handful of Tomatoes

I thought I could hold all four in one hand,
but I fumble, cursing
as one slips, hits the ground, splits.
Cradling the remaining orbs,
yellow, orange and red,
I snap a photo with my phone.
The picture so vibrant,
down to the pink flesh of my palm,
with an encouraging caption,
I send it to you,
my bright and brilliant friend,
hoping to lift your spirits.

I don't tell you
that the tomato branches bent,
succumbed to the weight of abundance,
dropping this precious fruit,
prematurely.

First Frost

After last night's freeze,
maple leaves are falling en masse
in our back yard,
draping shrubbery below
in a blanket of red,
insulating, protecting
from the next blast
of winter's icy breath.

It's raining red,
one species shedding its glory
to benefit another,
to share and protect what's fragile,
a transfusion.

Our neighborhood collects coats,
socks, gloves, caps for those
walking the streets this winter,
sleeping beneath the bridges
where warmth pools.
A church nearby is holding
a blood drive. No one likes
to be cold or cold-hearted.

The Lightness of Reprieve

Standing at our friend's threshold,
pockets padded with tissues,
we steel ourselves for heartache,
prepare to embrace longer than usual,
voice our true affections,
stutter through farewells.
To our surprise, she rallies,
rises from her sick bed,
responds to the attention,
the memories, the bonds we share.
Glancing back as we leave,
we see her waving from the doorway.

Later, we knock at the door of a cousin
recovering from a cardiac procedure.
She claims to feel ten years younger.
We fill this bonus time with laughter
and celebrate the lightness of reprieve.

Arriving home, we cringe to find
ruffled remains of a red-bellied
woodpecker, feathery outline still visible
on our glass door.
We gather its hollow form,
place it tenderly, respectfully,
in a shallow hole, hallowing
the fragility of life
at our own doorstep.

Attending to Grief

Beneath the beam of streetlights,
a young couple emerges from the darkness,
crossing our path:
he, tattooed, with a dimpled smile;
she, model lithe, clothes billowing.
Eyes drawn solely to our dog,
they ask her name.
Poppy, we say;
Poppy, they repeat, stooping
to pat her head, rub her fur,
gambol lightly with her in the grass.
He asks permission to give her
a treat, pulled from his pocket.
Odd, we think, that he would carry
such a thing. Poppy nuzzles them
like old friends, her knowing
attuned to their need.

We put our dog down
yesterday, they confess.
Our two cats remain, but
it's not the same.
We express condolences
less comforting than our dog's.

Last Leaf
(with a nod to O. Henry)

One final rusty leaf
clings to the dogwood tree
outside our bedroom window.
Resisting the wind's wrestling,
it beckons me back to a time
when I painted a single leaf
on our patio wall:
my Hail Mary attempt
to prolong the life of my father
as modern medicine failed,
as the leaves fell.

Desperate to bring him hope;
venturing outside the boundaries
of my own knowledge and faith,
I scheduled an appointment
with a local healer, Chief Two Trees.
But when travel became impossible,
I resorted to that lone leaf
and a no holds barred prayer.

After he died, I continued to paint,
self-medicating stroke by stroke,
adding to my winter wall-garden:
fern, forget-me-not, bleeding heart,
wisteria, live-for-ever;
each new leaf, petal, blossom,
balm to my wound.

Found in a Forest

Through the fog of a dream, I glimpse
them, not quite together yet,
but nearly so,
along a patch of woods I know well
from childhood, a grassy bank
ascending toward shadowed canopy.
The light behind the two, shimmering,
reveals outlines, but not features.
They are clearly my mother and father,
long gone to difficult deaths,
but now healthy and whole.
He runs along the upper line of woods; she below,
stepping out of shoes into cool grass.
Their reunion, so close;
I only need this dream once.

Crack in My Windshield

I recall the projectile's pop when it struck,
spun from a passing dump truck;
my startled response, gasping
from the shock of impact.

I can't pinpoint where we were,
when that niche,
a thin silver sliver began
to snake slowly down the glassy plate
like a meandering river.

Was it coming from the hospital on Tuesday,
where a cousin recovers;
or as we were returning
from Wednesday's visit with our cancer-laden
friend, afraid
this might be our last chance
to hug, to laugh, to reminisce?

I can't place its genesis,
but I do recognize a symbol
of heartbreak when I see it.
The windshield I can replace.

Mementoes

In a night-vision I met him again
as I stepped off a school bus
at Tallulah Gorge,
lowest point
east of the Mississippi.
This time as a dapper young man,
oxford button-down shirt,
crisp linen pants, dazzling white,
creased to perfection.
Who are you? I asked
this familiar stranger.

Pulling a weathered wallet
from his pocket,
he showed me pictures,
myself and my brothers as children,
mementoes of affection
only a father would carry.

Moravian Star

Freezing rain
glazes the Moravian Star
just beyond our front door,
crystal icicles stretching,
extending each point of light,
until it resembles a glowing comet,
tethered to earth like a kite.

Incandescent fireball
wind-tugs wildly at its electric mooring,
longing to unplug this world,
escape its hold and shoot skyward,
flinging icy particles as it climbs
to join its heavenly siblings.

Entranced by the star's dazzling dance,
I cheer for its escape,
to break its earthly bonds,
rise, and burn brighter still.

Marilyn Hedgpeth earned a BA in English from Salem College in Winston-Salem, NC, and an MDiv from Columbia Theological Seminary in Decatur, GA. She recently retired as a PC(USA) Minister of Word and Sacrament after preaching/teaching/leading/loving life through the church for 24 years. She has previously published sermons, adult curriculum, and articles for the Presbyterian Church, but this is her first published collection of poems. Marilyn and husband, Hedge, have three talented children (and spouses) and two grandchildren whom they adore. Having lived in Charlotte, Greensboro, Greenville, Atlanta and Durham for most of her life, she refers to I-85 as her home street, although she now calls Winston-Salem, NC home.

www.ingramcontent.com/pod-product-compliance
Lightning Source LLC
Chambersburg PA
CBHW040308170426
43194CB00022B/2948